Little People, BIG DREAMS®
MARIE CURIE

Written by
Maria Isabel Sánchez Vegara

Illustrated by
Frau Isa

Translated by Emma Martinez

Frances Lincoln
Children's Books

When Marie was a little girl, she made a vow to herself...
she was going to be a scientist, not a princess.

Marie was from a poor family but she was very smart. At school, she won a gold medal for her studies, which she kept in her drawer like a treasure.

Marie couldn't go to the same university as her brother. In her home country, only men were allowed to study. But she wouldn't take 'no' for an answer, so she packed her bags and moved away to France.

Even though studying in a new language was not easy, Marie soon became the best maths and science student in Paris!

One day, Marie met Pierre, and happily...
he loved science just like her.

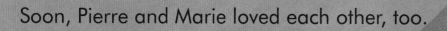

Soon, Pierre and Marie loved each other, too.

They married and became
Madame and Monsieur Curie!

Hidden away in their laboratory, Marie and Pierre discovered two incredible things: radium and polonium.

It was such a thrilling moment
for science!

They won a Nobel Prize for their research! Marie became the first woman to receive this honour.

One day, Pierre suffered a terrible accident, and
poor Marie was left alone.

Marie wiped her tears away and worked harder than ever.
The audience applauded loudly the day she was awarded
her second Nobel Prize.

A terrible war broke out. Marie's discoveries were used by doctors to help injured soldiers.

After the war was over, many girls followed in Marie's footsteps, studying at her Parisian institute.

She had valuable advice for every new student: in life, there is nothing to be afraid of, only many things to learn, and many ways to help those in need.

MARIE CURIE

(Born 1867 • Died 1934)

c.1869
(third from left)

1895

Marie Curie was born Maria Salomea Skłodowska in Warsaw, Poland. She is most famous for winning two Nobel Prizes – one for Physics, and one for Chemistry. She was the first female scientist to win a Nobel Prize, and the only female, so far, to win two in different subjects. She was a remarkable child, with an incredible love of learning. She overcame the loss of her mother at the age of ten to become a brilliant student. Despite Maria's talent, she wasn't allowed to go to the same university as her brother because she was a girl. She worked as a teacher, and a governess, before moving to Paris to study – where she became Marie. It was at this time that she

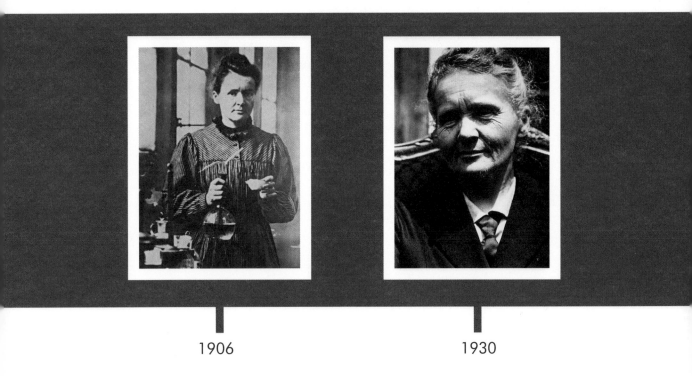

1906   1930

met Pierre Curie. They later married, and together, made the great scientific discovery of polonium and radium, and in 1903, they won the Nobel Prize for Physics. After the sudden loss of Pierre, who was killed in a road accident, Marie threw herself into work. She won a second Nobel Prize – this time for Chemistry – founded the Radium Institute at the University of Paris, and developed the use of X-rays to help injured soldiers in the First World War. Marie believed in the beauty of science, and that people would use science for good, not evil. She used all of her skills to search for knowledge, and her discoveries continue to help people with illnesses today.

Want to find out more about **Marie Curie**?
Have a read of these great books:

Who Was Marie Curie? by Megan Stine and Nancy Harrison
Women in Science: 50 Fearless Pioneers Who Changed the World by Rachel Ignotofsky
DK Biography: Marie Curie by Vicki Cobb
If you're in Paris, France, you could even visit the office and laboratory
of Marie Curie. Or experience a virtual tour here:
http://musee.curie.fr/visiter/visiteurs-individuels/visite-guidee

Brimming with creative inspiration, how-to projects, and useful information to enrich your everyday life, Quarto Knows is a favourite destination for those pursuing their interests and passions. Visit our site and dig deeper with our books into your area of interest: Quarto Creates, Quarto Cooks, Quarto Homes, Quarto Lives, Quarto Drives, Quarto Explores, Quarto Gifts, or Quarto Kids.

First published in the UK in 2017 by Frances Lincoln Children's Books, an imprint of The Quarto Group.
The Old Brewery, 6 Blundell Street, London N7 9BH, UK.
Visit our blogs at QuartoKnows.com

First published in Spain in 2016 under the title *Pequeña & Grande Marie Curie*
by Alba Editorial, s.l.u.
Baixada de Sant Miquel, 1, 08002 Barcelona, Spain. www.albaeditorial.es

A catalogue record for this book is available from the British Library.

UK ISBN 978-1-84780-961-2

Published by Rachel Williams • Designed by Andrew Watson
Edited by Katy Flint • Production by Dawn Cameron
Manufactured in Guangdong, China CC052021

Photographic acknowledgements (pages 28-29, from left to right) 1. Marie Curie as a young girl, c. 1869 © Lebrecht Music and
Arts Photo Library, Alamy Stock Photo 2. Marie and Pierre Curie, 1895 © AFP, Getty Images 3. Marie Curie, 1906 © Hulton Archive,
Getty Images 4. Portrait of Marie Curie, 1930 © Ewing Galloway, Alamy Stock Photo

Collect the *Little People,* **BIG DREAMS**® series:

FRIDA KAHLO	**COCO CHANEL**	**MAYA ANGELOU**	**AMELIA EARHART**	**AGATHA CHRISTIE**	**MARIE CURIE**	**ROSA PARKS**

AUDREY HEPBURN	**EMMELINE PANKHURST**	**ELLA FITZGERALD**	**ADA LOVELACE**	**JANE AUSTEN**	**GEORGIA O'KEEFFE**	**HARRIET TUBMAN**

ANNE FRANK	**MOTHER TERESA**	**JOSEPHINE BAKER**	**L. M. MONTGOMERY**	**JANE GOODALL**	**SIMONE DE BEAUVOIR**	**MUHAMMAD ALI**

STEPHEN HAWKING	**MARIA MONTESSORI**	**VIVIENNE WESTWOOD**	**MAHATMA GANDHI**	**DAVID BOWIE**	**WILMA RUDOLPH**	**DOLLY PARTON**

BRUCE LEE	**RUDOLF NUREYEV**	**ZAHA HADID**	**MARY SHELLEY**	**MARTIN LUTHER KING JR.**	**DAVID ATTENBOROUGH**	**ASTRID LINDGREN**

EVONNE GOOLAGONG	**BOB DYLAN**	**ALAN TURING**	**BILLIE JEAN KING**	**GRETA THUNBERG**	**JESSE OWENS**	**JEAN-MICHEL BASQUIAT**

ARETHA FRANKLIN

CORAZON AQUINO

PELÉ

ERNEST SHACKLETON

STEVE JOBS

AYRTON SENNA

LOUISE BOURGEOIS

ELTON JOHN

JOHN LENNON

PRINCE

CHARLES DARWIN

CAPTAIN TOM MOORE

HANS CHRISTIAN ANDERSEN

STEVIE WONDER

MEGAN RAPINOE

MARY ANNING

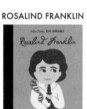

MALALA YOUSAFZAI

ANDY WARHOL

RUPAUL

MICHELLE OBAMA

MINDY KALING

IRIS APFEL

ROSALIND FRANKLIN

ACTIVITY BOOKS

STICKER ACTIVITY BOOK   COLOURING BOOK   LITTLE ME, BIG DREAMS JOURNAL

Discover more about the series at www.littlepeoplebigdreams.co.uk